MOM, I LOST MY JACKET

By Tynishia R. McGraw / Illustrated by Claude Harris

dedication
to my four, plus a nugget; love you always, and
way past forever.
xo, mom/yaya

Copyright © 2019 Tynishia R. McGraw

All rights reserved. No part of this publication may be reproduced, distributed, or transmitted in any form or by any means, including photocopying, recording, or other electronic or mechanical methods, without the prior written permission of the publisher, except in the case of brief quotations embodied in critical reviews and certain other noncommercial uses permitted by copyright law.

ISBN-13: 978-1-970079-25-8

Library of Congress:

Published by Opportune Independent Publishing Company

For permission requests, write to the publisher, addressed "Attention: Permissions Coordinator" to the address below.

Email: Info@opportunepublishing.com

Address: 113 N. Live Oak Street
Houston, TX 77003

Each day began with Riley's mom waking him up for school. It was still dark most times. He was never too happy to leave his warm bed.

He would always sit up, wrap his blanket around his body and stare into space. Riley really loved to sleep, so each school morning was very s...l...o...w moving.

Finally getting out of bed, he gets dressed in front of the warm hallway heater. He then makes his bed, nice and neat. Riley's stuffed "friends" are set up for the day ahead.

Vitamins—check! Brush teeth—check! Shoes on—check! Backpack—check! He is ready for school. Mom, Riley, and his brother Jordan head out the door.

Riley runs out the door, backpack in tow. He stops abruptly. "Mom, I forgot my jacket!" She shakes her head and hurries him back inside to put on his jacket. He is nice and warm now!

Every morning, the ride to school is filled with music. Riley loves music. He sings all the songs on the radio. It always makes the car ride seem very short. Sometimes, he has to read before the music. He does not like this very much.

Big brother Jordan is always dropped off first. He went to the high school just down the street from the elementary school. Riley is a 5th grader, and he enjoys school. He likes to be there early each morning to help with class breakfast.

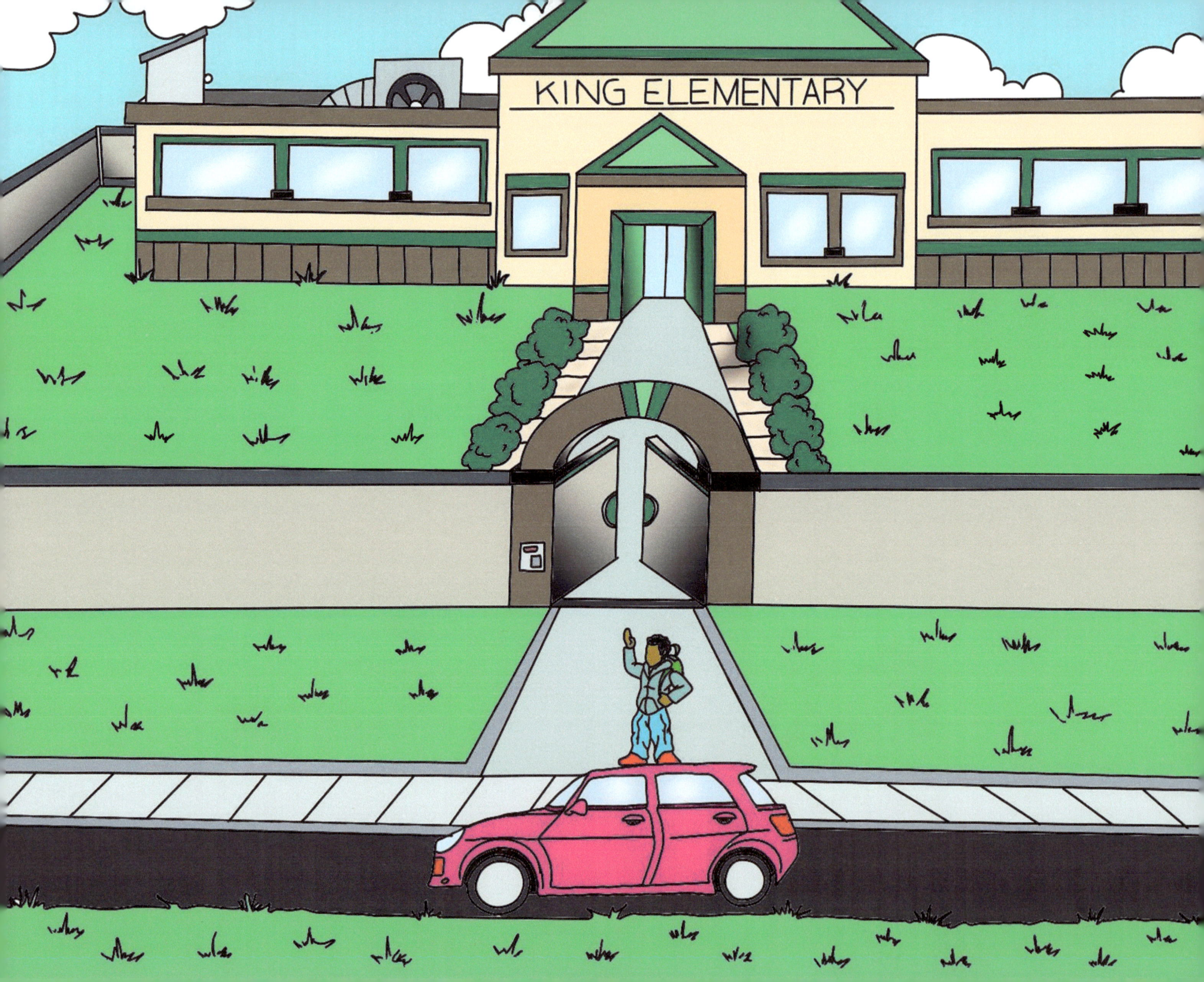

When his mom pulls up to the school, he hops out and races towards the gate. He hears his mom call after him, "Make sure you bring home your jacket." He yells back, "Ok Mom, I will!" He disappears around the corner into the school.

The school day goes quickly. Riley wears his jacket in the classroom most of the day because it is cool. At recess he gets warm, so he takes his jacket off and puts it on the fence.

The teacher calls for everyone to line up because recess is over. The students walk back into their classroom. They continue the daily work. Riley feels cool after a while. He gasps—Oh, no! He left his jacket on the fence outside! He must remember to get it before he goes home. Mom will be so upset if he forgets!

Riley finishes his last assignment of the day, and packs his homework in his book bag. He is excited to go home. His brother Jordan will be coming to pick him up so they can catch the train home. He arrives shortly after school is over. They head to the station.

They were almost there, when Jordan asks Riley where his jacket is. His eyes got really big, and he put his hand over his mouth. Oh no! He left it at school. He knows mom is going to be so upset. He is quiet the rest of the way home.

When the boys make it home, they call their mom to let her know. Mom asks to speak to Riley. She asks how his day was. He tells her it went great! Then before she could ask, he says, "Mom, I lost my jacket!" She is quiet, and says she will talk to him when she gets home. She reminds him to do his homework. He finishes up before she arrives.

When mom got home a little while later, she called for Riley as soon as she sat her purse down on the entry table. Riley looked up at her. He told her he would try to find his jacket tomorrow. She shakes her head and reminds him of how important it is to keep up with his belongings. After dinner, he gets ready for bed.

The next morning, Riley does his daily routine, and heads out the door with his mom and brother. He is thinking about finding his jacket. As soon as mom pulls up to the school, he jumps out and asks his mom to wait. He disappears inside the gate and around the corner. A couple minutes pass, and his smiling face appears. "Mom, I found my jacket!" She nods with approval. "Great job, Riley!" He grins widely. She tells him to make sure if he takes it off to put it in his bag.

Riley really works hard to keep up with his jacket for the rest of the school year. He makes sure to always take care of his belongings.

www.ingramcontent.com/pod-product-compliance
Lightning Source LLC
Chambersburg PA
CBHW040320100526
44583CB00004BB/162